Learning Is Fun GRADES K-1 Workbook

Modern Publishing
A Division of Unisystems, Inc.
New York, NY 10022

TO THE PARENTS

Dear Parents,

As your child's first and most important teacher, you can encourage your child's love of learning by participating in learning activities at home. Working together on the activities in this workbook will help your child build confidence, learn to reason, and develop reading, writing, math, language, and perception skills.

Following are some suggestions to help make your time together both enjoyable and rewarding.

● Choose a time when you and your child are relaxed.

● Provide a selection of writing material (either thick or thin pencils and/or crayons).

● Don't attempt to do too many pages at one time or expect that every page be completed. Move on if your child is frustrated or loses interest.

● Praise your child's efforts.

● Discuss each page. Help your child relate the concepts in this book to everyday experiences.

ESSENTIAL SKILLS

The repetitive activities within each chapter have been designed to help children learn to sort, separate, put together, and figure out—the organizational skills so necessary for learning and thinking.

CHAPTER 1 Handwriting Skills
Learning to control the small muscles of the hand **(fine motor skill development)** allows the child to make the precise movements necessary for forming letters, while activities such as **writing from left to right, tracing,** and **forming lines** help to refine **eye/hand coordination.** Making **associations**—recognizing what things "go together" (for example, a dog and a bone), enables a child to recognize that an upper case"A" and a lower case "a" go together.

CHAPTER 2 Colors, Shapes, and Numbers
Looking at familiar shapes helps children notice similarities and differences. Activities in which the child reproduces shapes and/or matches shapes to words, encourages sight vocabulary recognition and the ability to make **associations between words and objects.** Grouping things according to common attributes such as color, size, shape, etc. **(classification activities)**, encourages development of a child's ability to reason and make **logical connections. Recognizing number words, writing numerals,** and **forming sets of objects** all prepare a child for **basic math skills.**

CHAPTER 3 Basic Math Skills
Becoming familiar with the **order of numbers from 1 to 10, learning to write those numbers,** and **understanding the connection between a set of objects and its corresponding numeral,** all prepare a child to understand the concepts of addition and subtraction.

CHAPTER 4 Reading Readiness
Determining which items in a group "go together" **(making associations)**, and learning to group things according to common attributes **(classification skills)**, prepare a child to **notice details**. These skills are necessary for learning to recognize and reproduce the letters of the alphabet.

CHAPTER 5 Phonics Skills I
This chapter focuses on teaching a child to **recognize the initial and final consonant sounds, to learn to write letters and words using these sounds,** and **to understand the association between sounds, symbols, and words.**

CHAPTER 6 Phonics Skills II
Phonics II focuses on training a child to **hear and reproduce the long and short vowel sounds**, as well as the sounds made by combining two letters to make **consonant blends.**

TABLE OF CONTENTS

HANDWRITING SKILLS

Trace the broken lines.

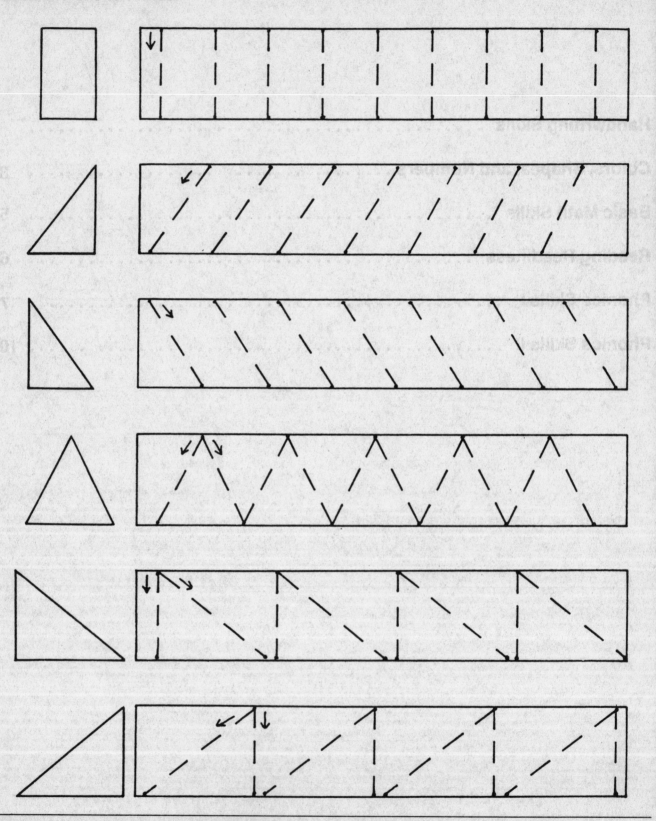

Skills: Fine motor skill development; Forming vertical and diagonal lines; Eye/hand coordination; Corresponding relationships

HANDWRITING SKILLS

Trace the broken lines.

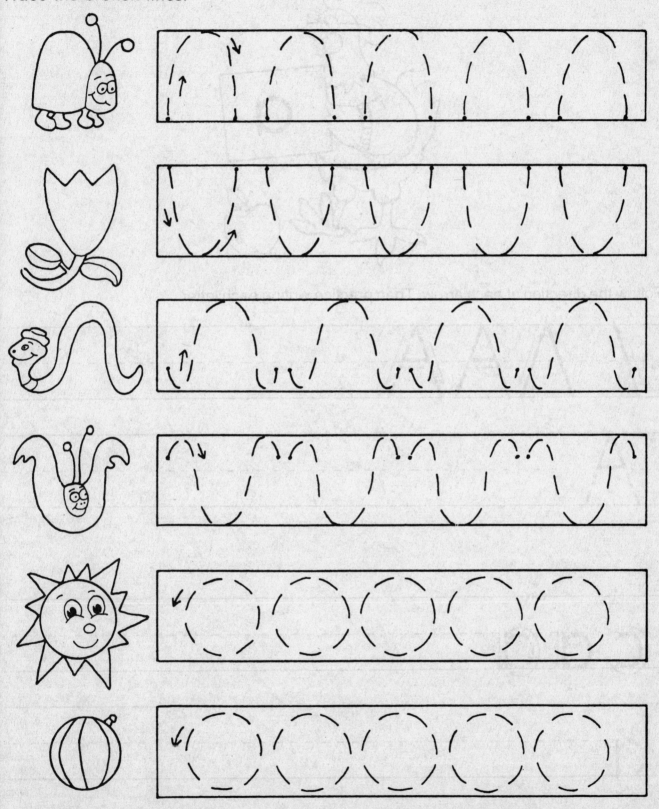

Skills: Fine motor skill development; Eye/hand coordination; Corresponding relationships

HANDWRITING SKILLS

Follow the direction of each arrow. Then practice writing each letter.

Skills: Forming upper/lower case "a"; Writing left to right

HANDWRITING SKILLS

Follow the direction of each arrow. Then practice writing each letter.

Skills: Forming upper/lower case "b"; Writing left to right

HANDWRITING SKILLS

Follow the direction of each arrow. Then practice writing each letter.

Skills: Forming upper/lower case "c"; Writing left to right

HANDWRITING SKILLS

Follow the direction of each arrow. Then practice writing each letter.

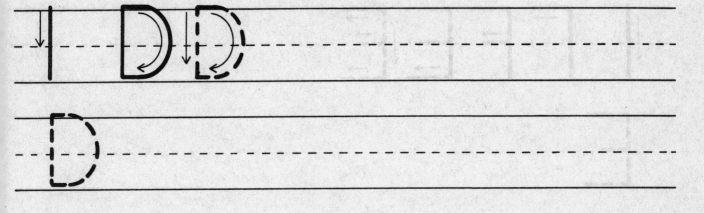

Skills: Forming upper/lower case "d"; Writing left to right

HANDWRITING SKILLS

Follow the direction of each arrow. Then practice writing each letter.

Skills: Forming upper/lower case "e"; Writing left to right

HANDWRITING SKILLS

Follow the direction of each arrow. Then practice writing each letter.

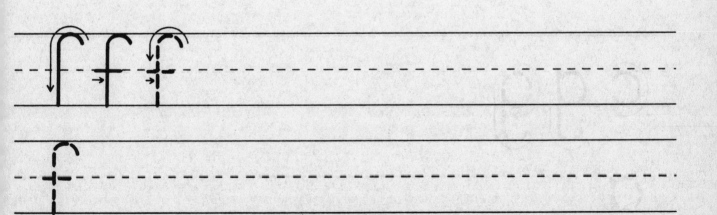

Skills: Forming upper/lower case "f"; Writing left to right

HANDWRITING SKILLS

Follow the direction of each arrow. Then practice writing each letter.

Skills: Forming upper/lower case "g"; Writing left to right

HANDWRITING SKILLS

Follow the direction of each arrow. Then practice writing each letter.

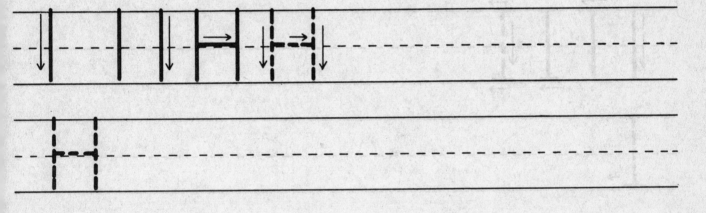

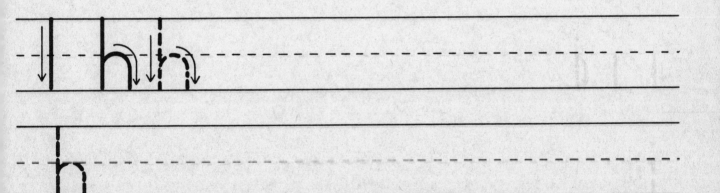

Skills: Forming upper/lower case "h"; Writing left to right

HANDWRITING SKILLS

Follow the direction of each arrow. Then practice writing each letter.

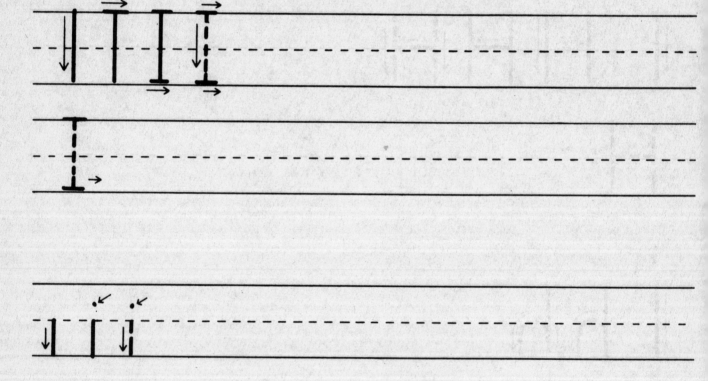

Skills: Forming upper/lower case "i"; Writing left to right

Follow the direction of each arrow. Then practice writing each letter.

Skills: Forming upper/lower case "j"; Writing left to right

HANDWRITING SKILLS

Follow the direction of each arrow. Then practice writing each letter.

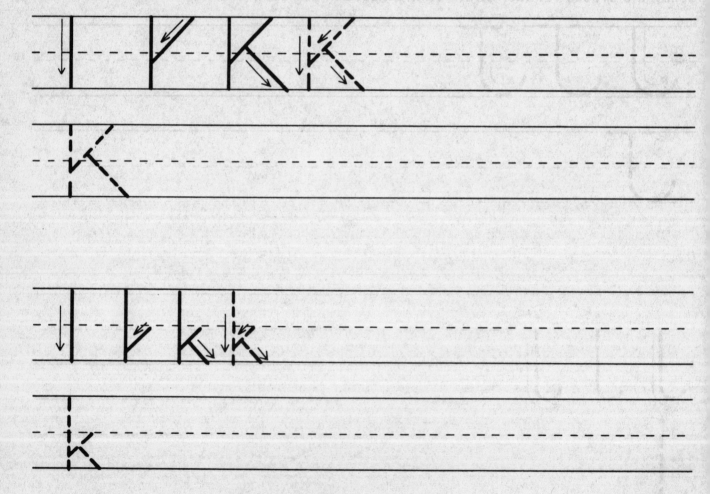

Skills: Forming upper/lower case "k"; Writing left to right

HANDWRITING SKILLS

Follow the direction of each arrow. Then practice writing each letter.

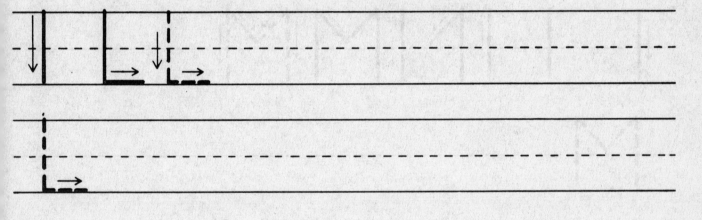

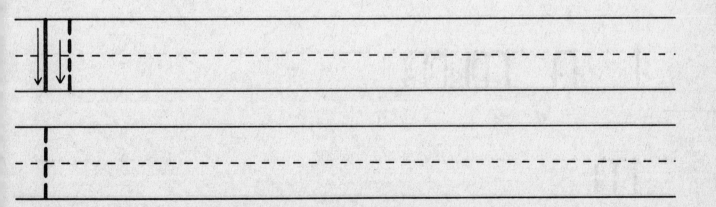

Skills: Forming upper/lower case "l"; Writing left to right

HANDWRITING SKILLS

Follow the direction of each arrow. Then practice writing each letter.

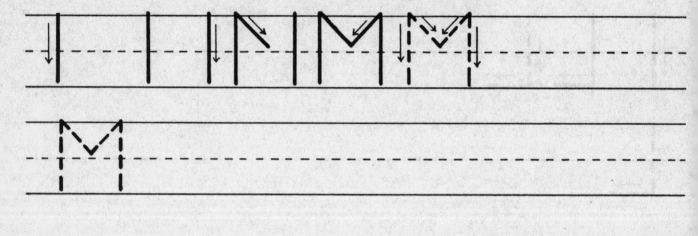

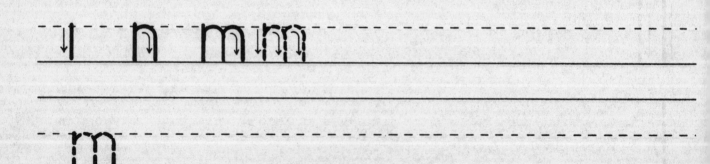

Skills: Forming upper/lower case "m"; Writing left to right

HANDWRITING SKILLS

Follow the direction of each arrow. Then practice writing each letter.

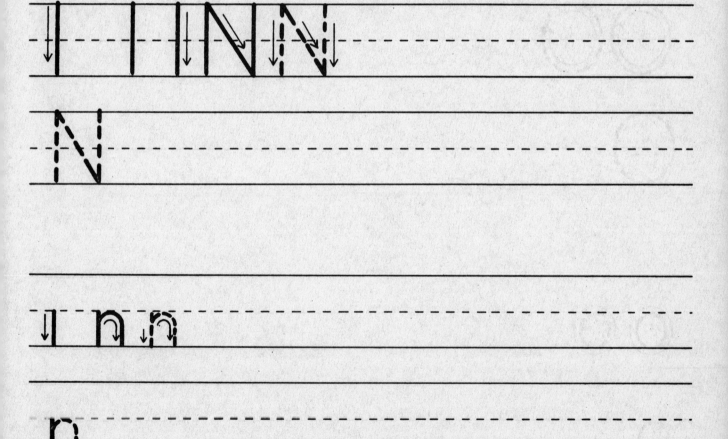

Skills: Forming upper/lower case "n"; Writing left to right

HANDWRITING SKILLS

Follow the direction of each arrow. Then practice writing each letter.

Skills: Forming upper/lower case "o"; Writing left to right

Follow the direction of each arrow. Then practice writing each letter.

Skills: Forming upper/lower case "p"; Writing left to right

HANDWRITING SKILLS

Follow the direction of each arrow. Then practice writing each letter.

Skills: Forming upper/lower case "q"; Writing left to right

HANDWRITING SKILLS

Follow the direction of each arrow. Then practice writing each letter.

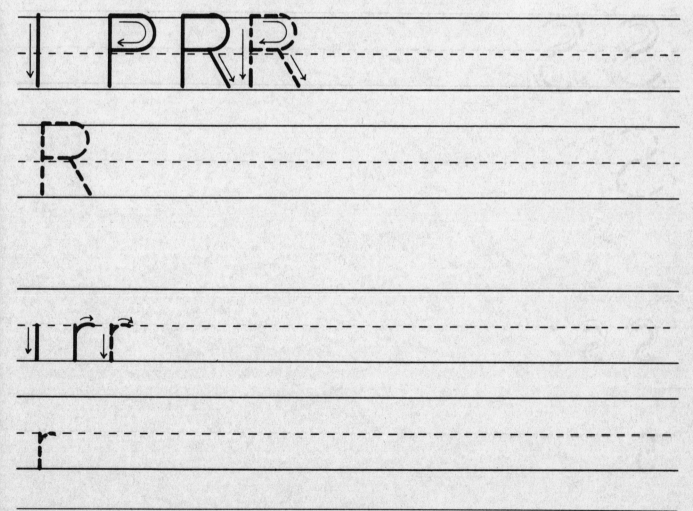

Skills: Forming upper/lower case "r"; Writing left to right

HANDWRITING SKILLS

Follow the direction of each arrow. Then practice writing each letter.

Skills: Forming upper/lower case "s"; Writing left to right

HANDWRITING SKILLS

Follow the direction of each arrow. Then practice writing each letter.

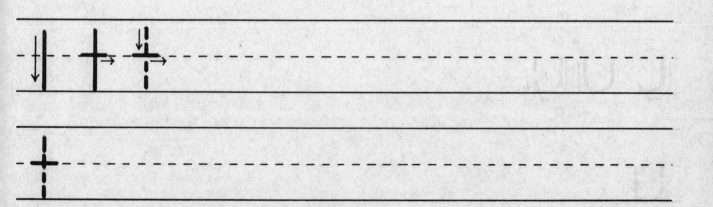

Skills: Forming upper/lower case "t"; Writing left to right

HANDWRITING SKILLS

Follow the direction of each arrow. Then practice writing each letter.

Skills: Forming upper/lower case "u"; Writing left to right

HANDWRITING SKILLS

Follow the direction of each arrow. Then practice writing each letter.

Skills: Forming upper/lower case "v"; Writing left to right

HANDWRITING SKILLS

Follow the direction of each arrow. Then practice writing each letter.

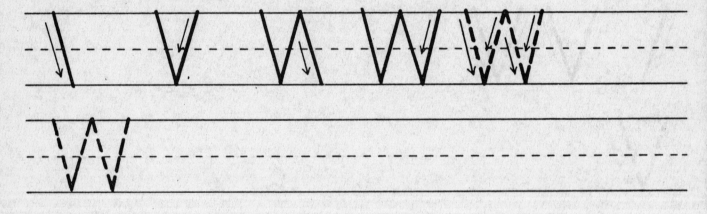

Skills: Forming upper/lower case "w"; Writing left to right

HANDWRITING SKILLS

Follow the direction of each arrow. Then practice writing each letter.

Skills: Forming upper/lower case "x"; Writing left to right

HANDWRITING SKILLS

Follow the direction of each arrow. Then practice writing each letter.

Skills: Forming upper/lower case "y"; Writing left to right

HANDWRITING SKILLS

Follow the direction of each arrow. Then practice writing each letter.

Skills: Forming upper/lower case "z"; Writing left to right

red red r

Color these things that are red.

Skills: Distinguishing color; Classification; Word recognition

COLORS, SHAPES, AND NUMBERS

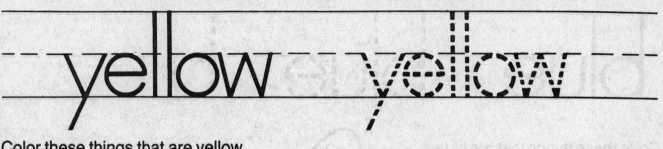

Color these things that are yellow.

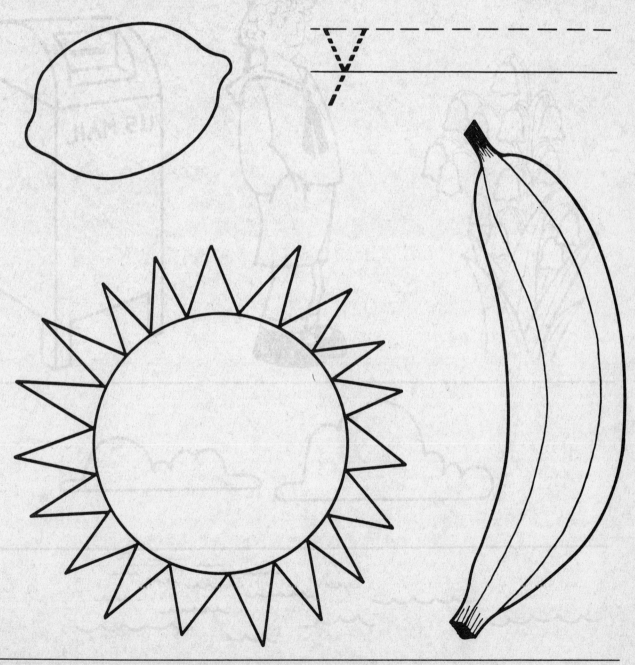

Skills: Distinguishing color; Classification; Word recognition

blue   blue   b

Color these things that are blue.

Skills: Distinguishing color; Classification; Word recognition

orange   orange

O

Color these things that are orange.

Skills: Distinguishing color; Classification; Word recognition

COLORS, SHAPES, AND NUMBERS

purple purple

p

Color these things that are purple.

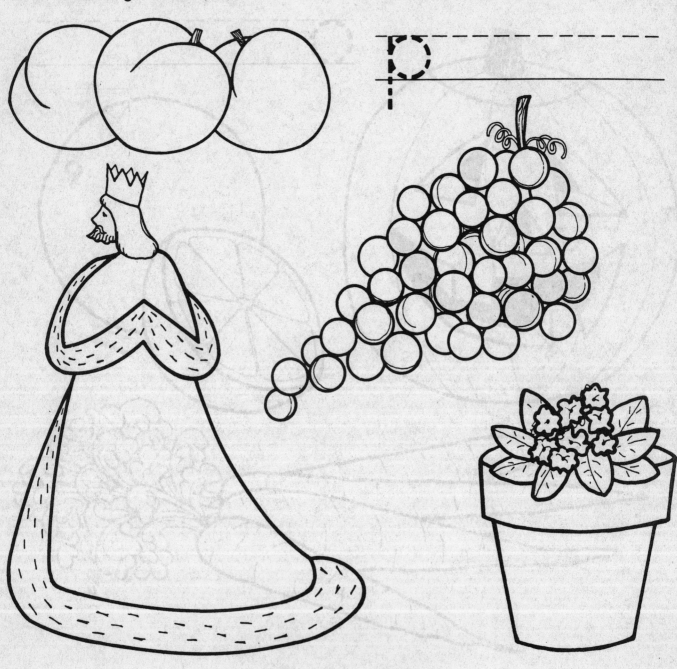

Skills: Distinguishing color; Classification; Word recognition

green green

Color these things that are green.

g

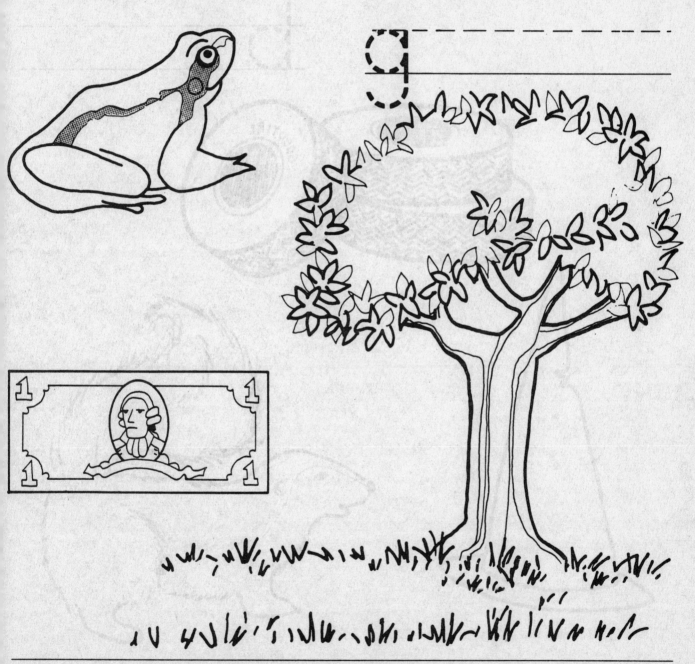

Skills: Distinguishing color; Classification; Word recognition

black   black

Color these things that are black.

b

Skills: Distinguishing color; Classification; Word recognition

brown   brown

b

Color these things that are brown.

Skills: Distinguishing color; Classification; Word recognition

COLORS, SHAPES, AND NUMBERS

Look at the square.
Then trace, print, and draw.

square

square

s

Draw 1 big square.
Color it red.

Draw 1 small square.
Color it blue.

Skills: Fine motor skill development; Sight vocabulary recognition; Association between sight vocabulary and shapes

COLORS, SHAPES, AND NUMBERS

Look at the circle.
Then trace, print, and draw.

circle

circle

Draw 1 big circle.
Color it green.

Draw 1 small circle.
Color it brown.

Skills: Fine motor skill development; Sight vocabulary recognition; Association between sight vocabulary and shapes

COLORS, SHAPES, AND NUMBERS

Look at the rectangle.
Then trace, print, and draw.

rectangle

rectangle

Draw 1 big rectangle.
Color it yellow.

Draw 1 small rectangle.
Color it black.

Skills: Fine motor skill development; Sight vocabulary recognition; Association between sight vocabulary and shapes

COLORS, SHAPES, AND NUMBERS

Look at the triangle.
Then trace, print, and draw.

triangle

triangle

Draw 1 big triangle.
Color it green.

Draw 1 small triangle.
Color it blue.

Skills: Fine motor skill development; Sight vocabulary recognition; Association between sight vocabulary and shapes

COLORS, SHAPES, AND NUMBERS

Circle the correct numeral.

(7)   6   9

2   3   8

2   8   3

7   3   1

9   10   6

2   5   6

9   4   8

2   4   10

4   3   5

6   9   2

Skills: Recognizing sets of objects and the corresponding numeral; Following directions

COLORS, SHAPES, AND NUMBERS

Print the correct numeral.

3

COLORS, SHAPES, AND NUMBERS

Circle the correct word.

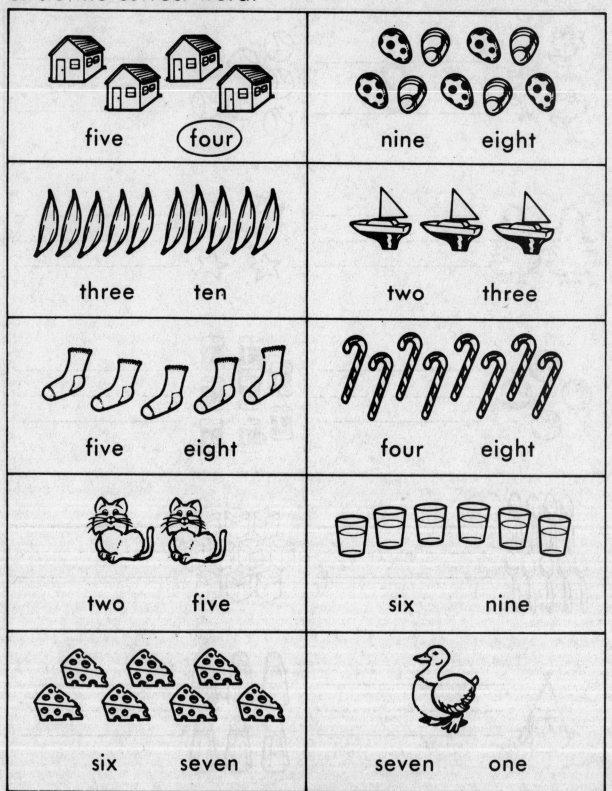

five   (four)

nine   eight

three   ten

two   three

five   eight

four   eight

two   five

six   nine

six   seven

seven   one

Skills: Recognizing sets of objects and the corresponding number word

COLORS, SHAPES, AND NUMBERS

Trace the word. Print the numeral. Draw the correct number of circles.

one   1   ◯

eight

six

three

seven

Skills: Recognizing number words and writing numerals; Forming corresponding sets of objects

COLORS, SHAPES, AND NUMBERS

Trace the word. Print the numeral. Draw the correct number of circles.

four 4   ○ ○ ○ ○

two

ten

nine

five

Skills: Recognizing number words and writing numerals; Forming corresponding sets of objects

BASIC MATH SKILLS

Look at each book.
What number comes next?

8 | 9

6 | ___

2 | ___

7 | ___

4 | ___

9 | ___

5 | ___

3 | ___

Skills: Ordering numbers to 10; Writing numerals

BASIC MATH SKILLS

Look at each group of ice cream cones.
What number comes between?

Skills: Ordering numbers to 10; Writing numerals

BASIC MATH SKILLS

Look at each group of apples.
Write the missing numbers.

Skills: Ordering numbers to 10; Writing numerals

BASIC MATH SKILLS

Look at each picture.
How many are in the first group?

How many are in the second group?
How many in all?

$\underline{2}$ and $\underline{1}$ is $\underline{3}$

_____   and   _____   is   _____

_____   and   _____   is   _____

Skills: Recognizing sets of objects and writing corresponding numerals; Adding groups of objects

BASIC MATH SKILLS

Look at each picture.
How many are in the first group?

How many are in the second group?
How many in all?

_____ and _____ is _____

_____ and _____ is _____

_____ and _____ is _____

Skills: Recognizing sets of objects and writing corresponding numerals; Adding groups of objects

BASIC MATH SKILLS

Look at each picture.
How many are in the first group?

How many are in the second group?
How many in all?

$$\underline{3}$$ and $$\underline{1}$$ is $$\underline{4}$$

$$\underline{3}$$ + $$\underline{1}$$ = $$\underline{4}$$

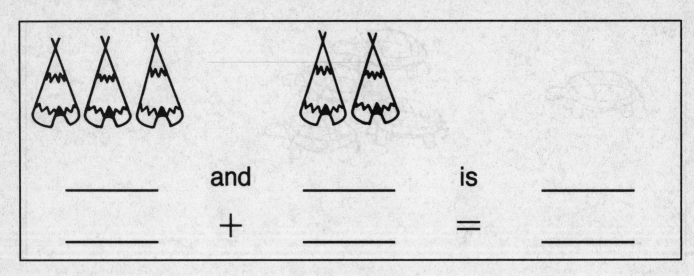

_____ and _____ is _____

_____ + _____ = _____

_____ and _____ is _____

_____ + _____ = _____

Skills: Recognizing sets of objects and writing corresponding numerals; Adding groups of objects; Understanding addition sentences

56

BASIC MATH SKILLS

Look at each picture.
How many are in the first group?

How many are in the second group?
How many in all?

_____ + _____ = _____

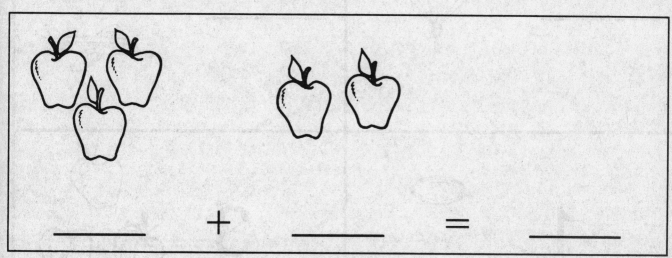

_____ + _____ = _____

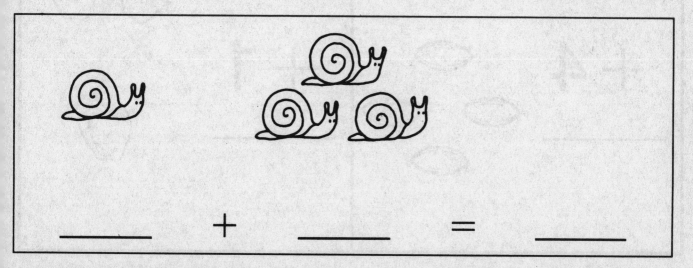

_____ + _____ = _____

Skills: Recognizing sets of objects and writing corresponding numerals; Adding groups of objects; Practicing addition problems

BASIC MATH SKILLS

How many in all?
Add to find out.

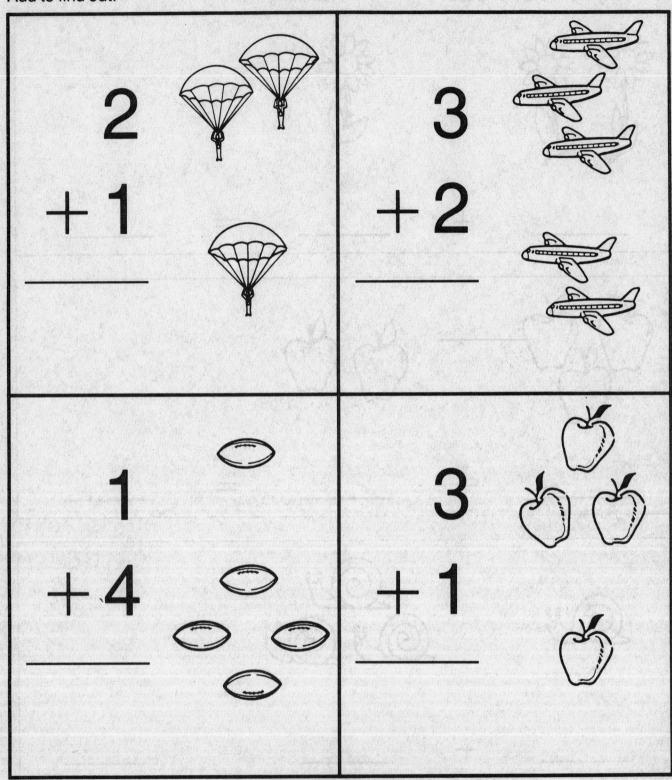

Skills: Solving vertical addition problems; Writing numerals

BASIC MATH SKILLS

How many in all?
Add to find out.

$$\begin{array}{r} 7 \\ +\,3 \\ \hline \end{array}$$

$$\begin{array}{r} 4 \\ +\,5 \\ \hline \end{array}$$

$$\begin{array}{r} 2 \\ +\,4 \\ \hline \end{array}$$

$$\begin{array}{r} 5 \\ +\,3 \\ \hline \end{array}$$

Skills: Solving vertical addition problems to 10; Writing numerals

BASIC MATH SKILLS

Look at each picture.
How many are left?

__3__ take away __1__ is __2__

__5__ take away _____ is _____

__4__ take away _____ is _____

Skills: Recognizing sets of objects and writing corresponding numerals; Subtracting groups of objects

BASIC MATH SKILLS

Look at each picture.
How many are left?

5 take away _____ is _____

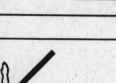

4 take away _____ is _____

2 take away _____ is _____

Skills: Recognizing sets of objects and writing corresponding numerals; Subtracting groups of objects

BASIC MATH SKILLS

Look at each picture.
How many are left?

| 5 | take away | _____ | is | _____ |
| 5 | − | _____ | = | _____ |

| 3 | take away | _____ | is | _____ |
| 3 | − | _____ | = | _____ |

| 4 | take away | _____ | is | _____ |
| 4 | − | _____ | = | _____ |

Skills: Recognizing sets of objects and writing corresponding numerals; Subtracting groups of objects; Understanding subtraction sentences

BASIC MATH SKILLS

Look at each picture.
How many are left?

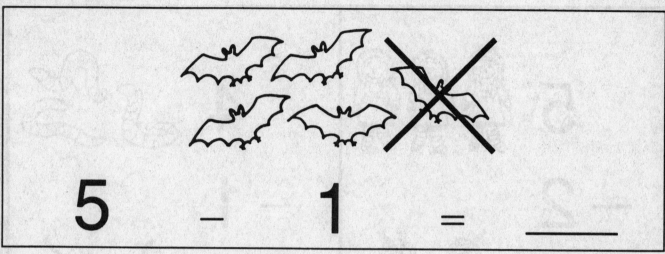

$$5 \quad - \quad 1 \quad = \quad \underline{}$$

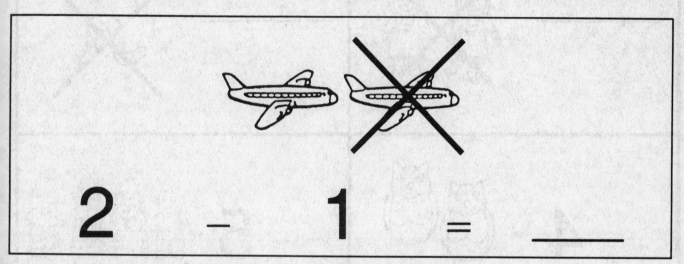

$$2 \quad - \quad 1 \quad = \quad \underline{}$$

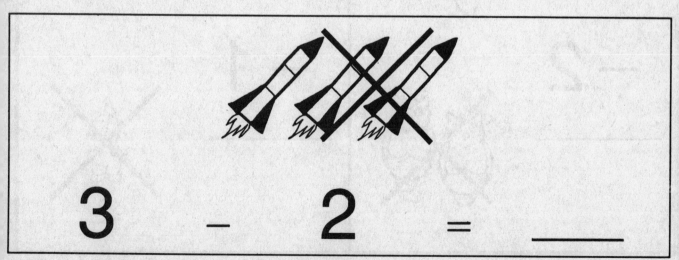

$$3 \quad - \quad 2 \quad = \quad \underline{}$$

Skills: Recognizing sets of objects and writing corresponding numerals; Subtracting groups of objects; Practicing subtraction problems

BASIC MATH SKILLS

Look at each picture.
How many are left?

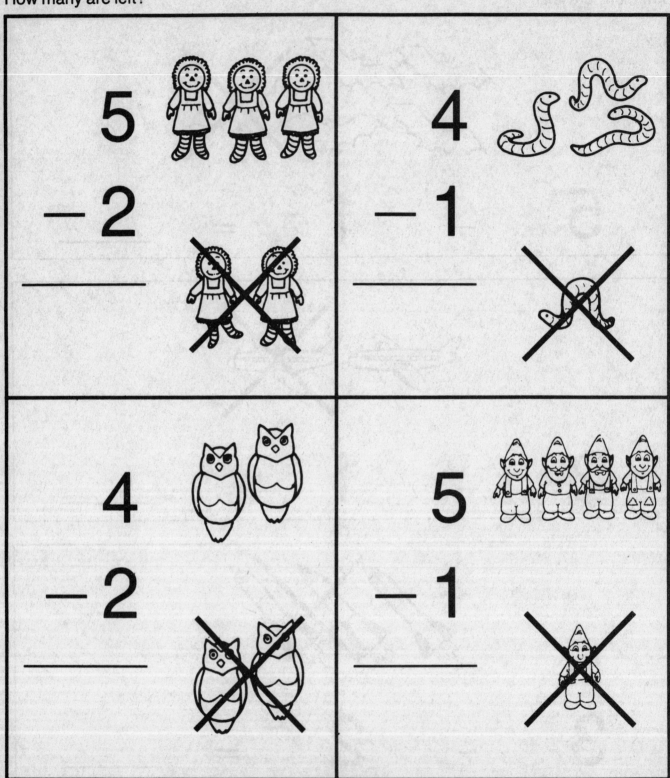

Skills: Solving vertical subtraction problems; Writing numerals

BASIC MATH SKILLS

How many are left?
Subtract to find out.

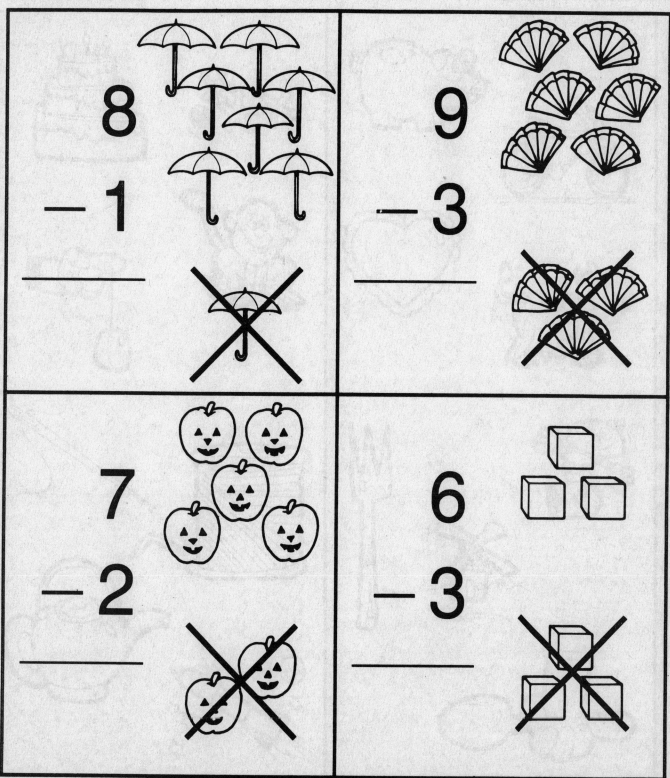

READING READINESS

Color the two pictures in each box that go together.

Skills: Association; Classification; Logical reasoning

READING READINESS

Look at the pictures in each row.
Cross out the one that is different.
Then color the others.

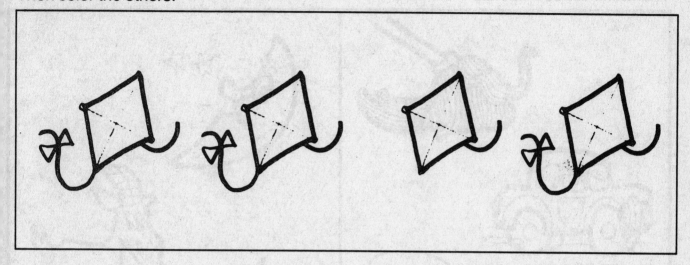

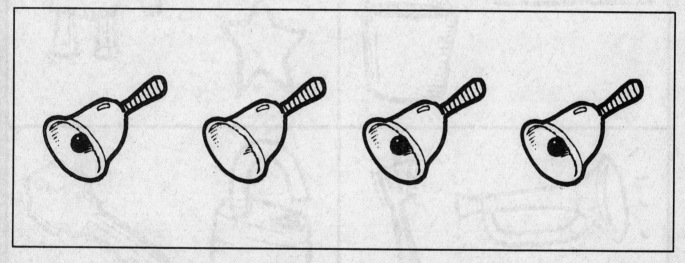

Skills: Visual discrimination; Noticing details

READING READINESS

Which one does not belong?
Cross out the one that does not belong with the others.
Then color the other pictures.

Skills: Classification; Association

READING READINESS

Look at the large pictures.
Then look at the detail in each small box.

Find the detail in each large picture and circle it.
Then color the pictures.

Skills: Visual discrimination; Noticing details

READING READINESS

Look at the first picture in each row and say its name.
Circle the picture whose name rhymes with it.

Skills: Auditory discrimination; Reproducing sounds

READING READINESS

Look at the pattern in each row.
Draw a line to the picture that continues each pattern.
Then color the pictures.

Skills: Observing and continuing patterns; Visual memory

READING READINESS

Look at the pattern in each row.
Draw a line to the picture that continues each pattern.
Then color the pictures.

Skills: Observing and continuing patterns; Visual memory

READING READINESS

Look at the pattern in each row.
Draw a line to the picture that continues each pattern.
Then color the pictures.

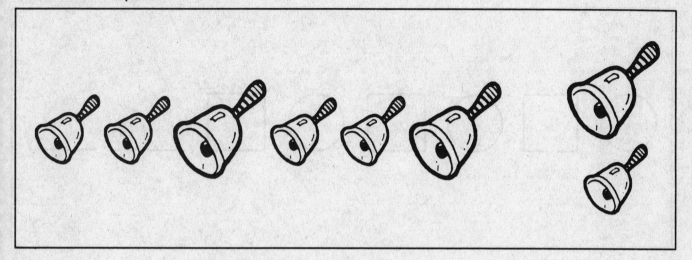

Skills: Observing and continuing patterns; Visual memory; Size discrimination

READING READINESS

Look at the pattern in each row.
Draw pictures to continue the pattern.
Then color the shapes.

○ □ ○ □ ○ □ ___ ___

□ △ ○ □ △ ○ ___ ___

□ □ ○ □ □ ○ ___ ___

Skills: Observing and reproducing patterns; Visual memory; Fine motor skill development

PHONICS SKILLS I

Initial consonant: **b**

Print the letters and words.

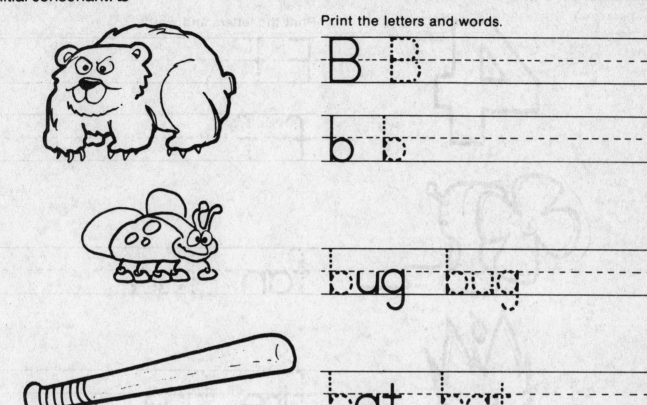

Finish the picture. Finish the word.

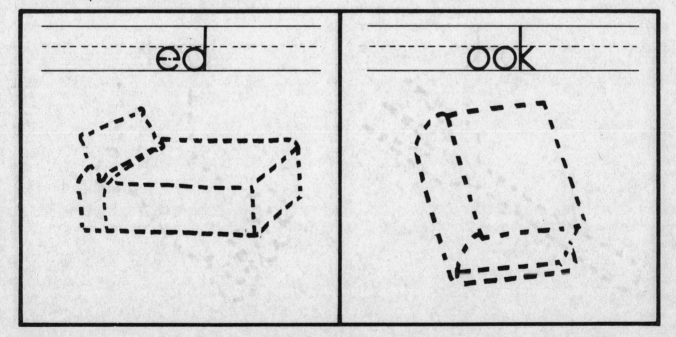

Skills: Recognition of the initial consonant "b"; Writing letters and words; Association between sounds, symbols, and words

PHONICS SKILLS I

Initial consonant: **f**

Print the letters and words.

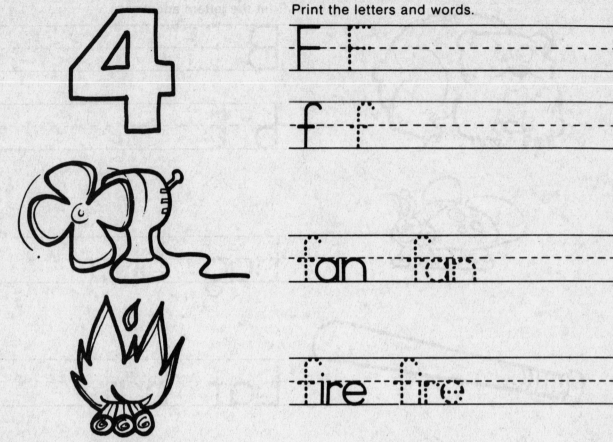

F F

f f

fan fan

fire fire

Finish the picture. Finish the word.

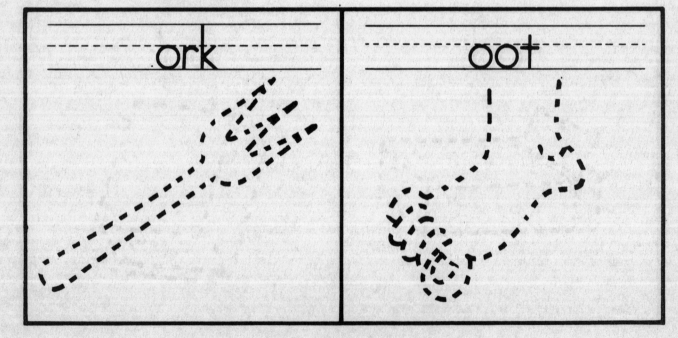

ork

oot

Skills: Recognition of the initial consonant "f"; Writing letters and words; Association between sounds, symbols, and words

PHONICS SKILLS I

Initial consonant: **g**

Print the letters and words.

G G

g g

goat goat

gate gate

Finish the picture. Finish the word.

ir

as

Skills: Recognition of the initial consonant "g"; Writing letters and words; Association between sounds, symbols, and words

PHONICS SKILLS I

Initial consonant: **k**

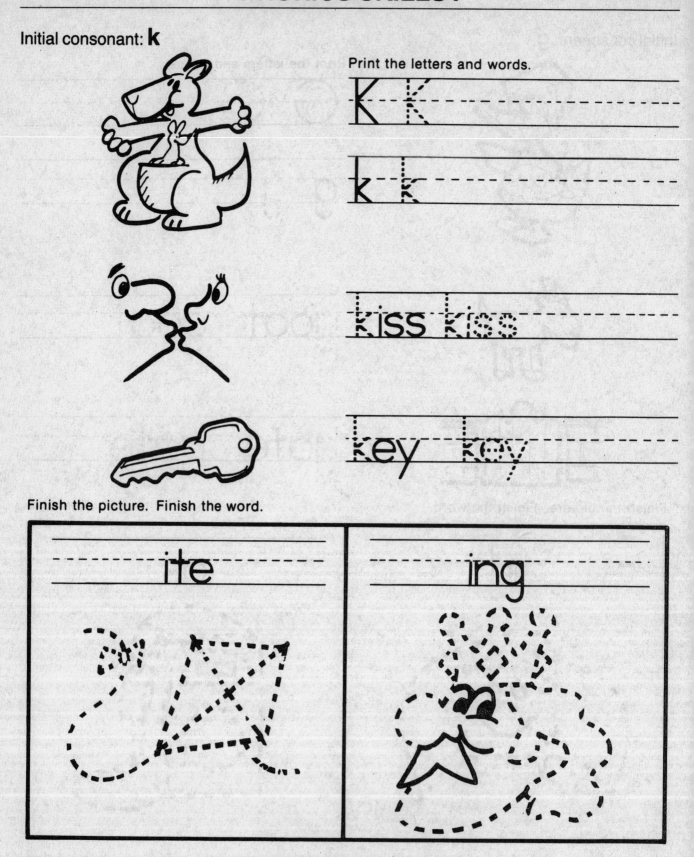

Print the letters and words.

K   K

k   k

kiss kiss

key   key

Finish the picture. Finish the word.

_ _ _ ite

_ _ _ ing

Skills: Recognition of the initial consonant "k"; Writing letters and words; Association between sounds, symbols, and words

Initial consonant: **V**

Print the letters and words.

V   V

v   v

vine   vine

van   van

Finish the picture. Finish the word.

est

ase

Skills: Recognition of the initial consonant "v"; Writing letters and words; Association between sounds, symbols, and words

PHONICS SKILLS I

Initial consonant: **C**

Print the letters and words.

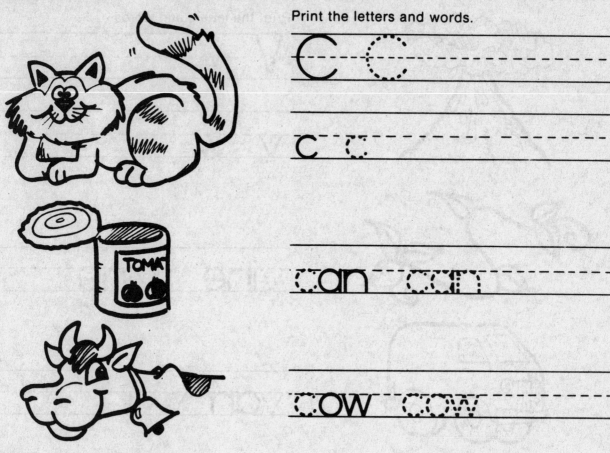

C C

c c

can can

cow cow

Finish the picture. Finish the word.

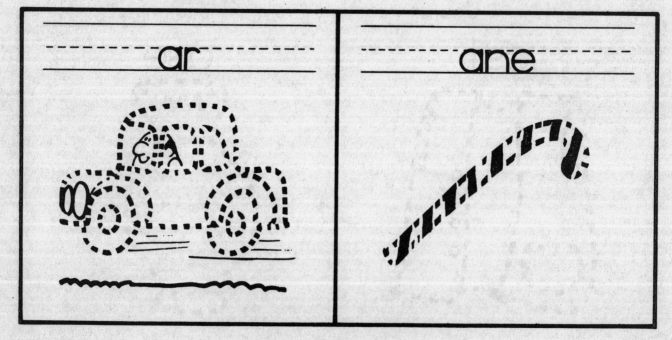

ar

ane

Skills: Recognition of the initial consonant "c"; Writing letters and words; Association between sounds, symbols, and words

PHONICS SKILLS I

Initial consonant: **h**

Print the letters and words.

H H

h h

hive hive

hat hat

Finish the picture. Finish the word.

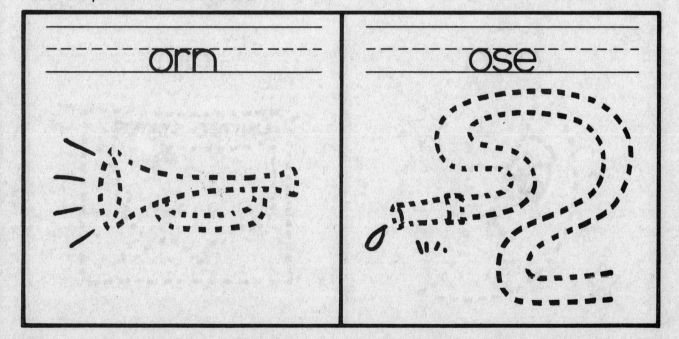

orn

ose

Skills: Recognition of the initial consonant "h"; Writing letters and words; Association between sounds, symbols, and words

PHONICS SKILLS I

Initial consonant: **m**

Print the letters and words.

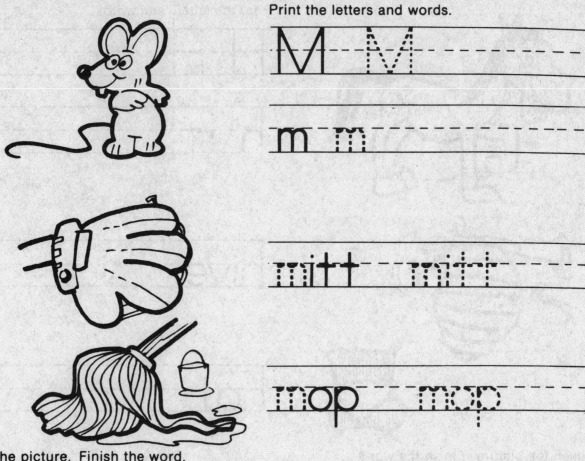

M M

m m

mitt mitt

mop mop

Finish the picture. Finish the word.

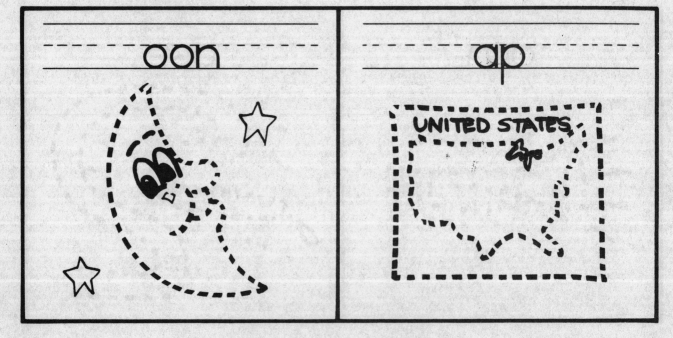

oon

ap

UNITED STATES

Skills: Recognition of the initial consonant "m"; Writing letters and words; Association between sounds, symbols, and words

PHONICS SKILLS I

Initial consonant: **p**

Print the letters and words.

P P

p p

pig pig

pin pin

Finish the picture. Finish the word.

eas

ie

Skills: Recognition of the initial consonant "p"; Writing letters and words; Association between sounds, symbols, and words

Initial consonant: y

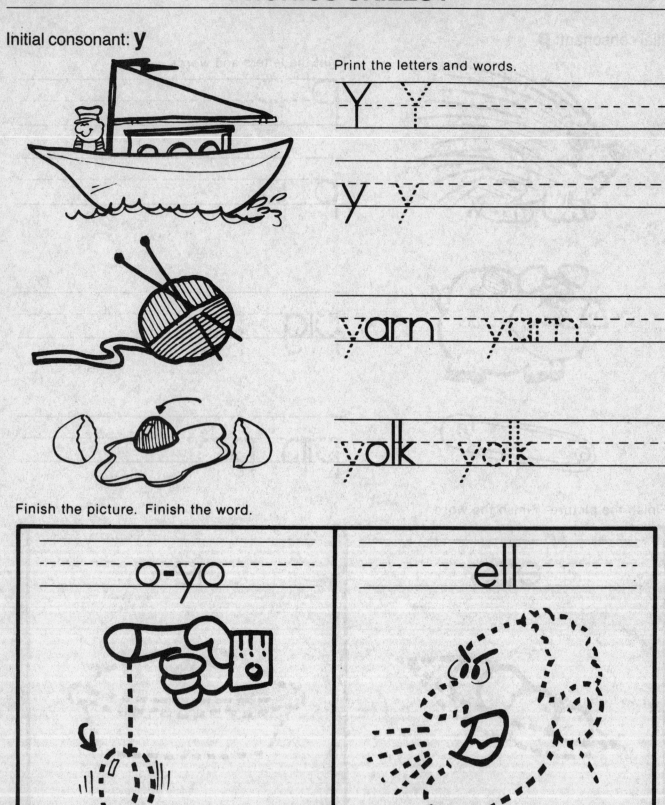

Print the letters and words.

Y Y

y y

yarn yarn

yolk yolk

Finish the picture. Finish the word.

o-yo

ell

Skills: Recognition of the initial consonant "y"; Writing letters and words; Association between sounds, symbols, and words

PHONICS SKILLS I

Initial consonant: **d**

Print the letters and words.

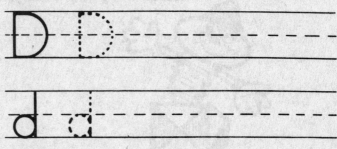

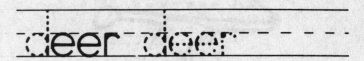

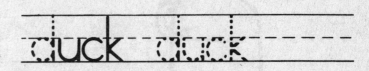

Finish the picture. Finish the word.

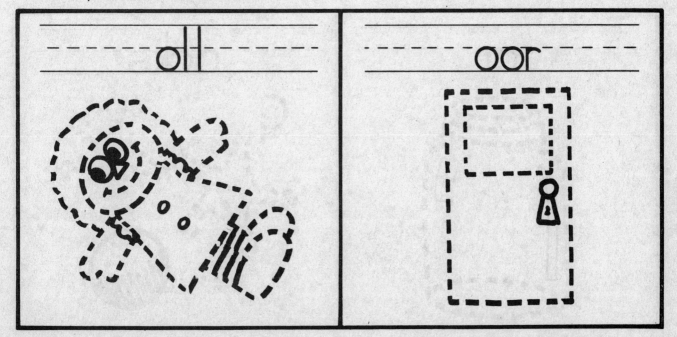

Skills: Recognition of the initial consonant "d"; Writing letters and words; Association between sounds, symbols, and words

85

PHONICS SKILLS I

Initial consonant: **j**

Print the letters and words.

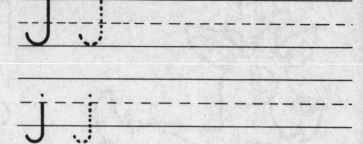

J J

j j

jet jet

jug jug

Finish the picture. Finish the word.

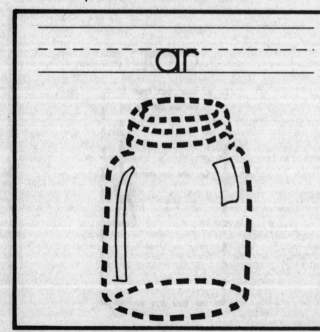

ar

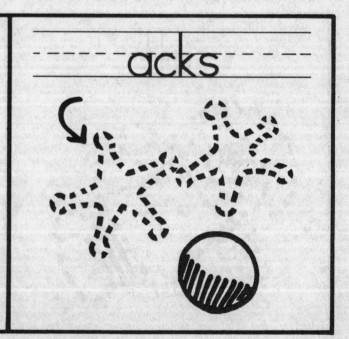

acks

Skills: Recognition of the initial consonant "j"; Writing letters and words; Association between sounds, symbols, and words

PHONICS SKILLS I

Initial consonant: **l**

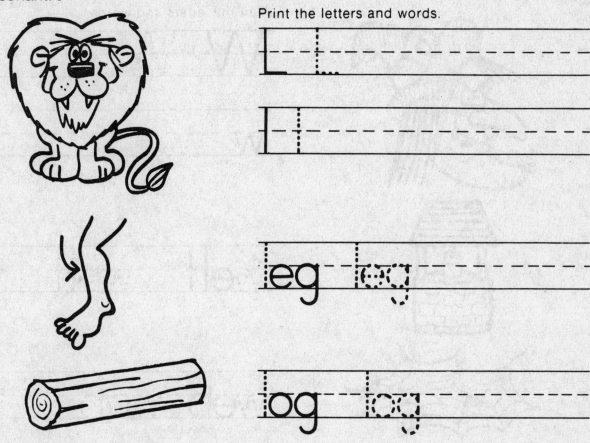

Print the letters and words.

leg leg

log log

Finish the picture. Finish the word.

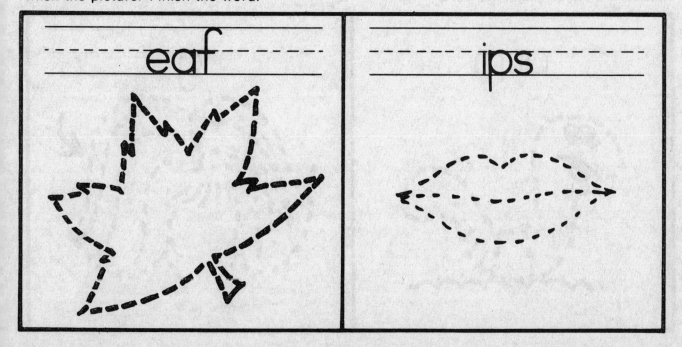

eaf

ips

Skills: Recognition of the initial consonant "l"; Writing letters and words; Association between sounds, symbols, and words

PHONICS SKILLS I

Initial consonant: W

Print the letters and words.

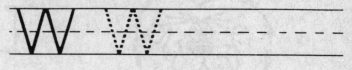

W W

w w

well well

web web

Finish the picture. Finish the word.

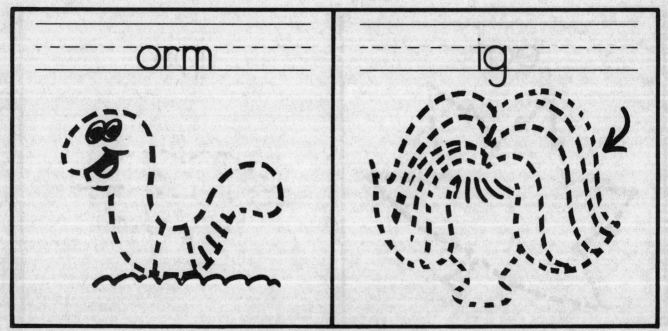

___orm

___ig

Skills: Recognition of the initial consonant "w"; Writing letters and words; Association between sounds, symbols, and words

PHONICS SKILLS I

Initial consonant: **Z**

Print the letters and words.

Z Z

z z

ZOO ZOO

zero zero

Finish the picture. Finish the word.

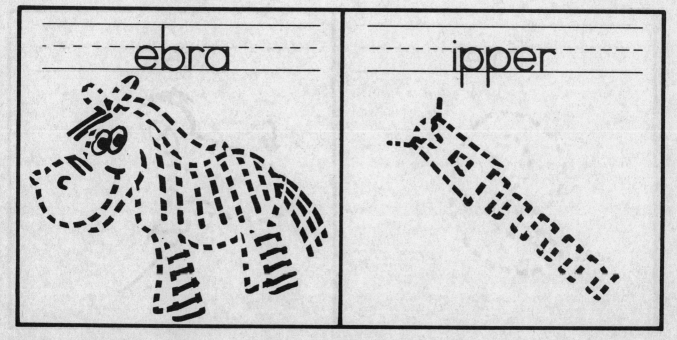

_ebra

_ipper

Skills: Recognition of the initial consonant "z"; Writing letters and words; Association between sounds, symbols, and words

PHONICS SKILLS I

Initial consonant: **n**

Print the letters and words.

N N

n n

nut nut

net net

Finish the picture. Finish the word.

ine

ose

Skills: Recognition of the initial consonant "n"; Writing letters and words; Association between sounds, symbols, and words

PHONICS SKILLS I

Initial consonant: q

Print the letters and words.

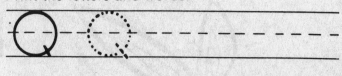

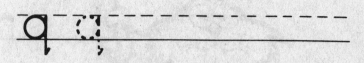

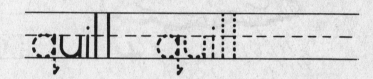

Finish the picture. Finish the word.

Skills: Recognition of the initial consonant "q"; Writing letters and words; Association between sounds, symbols, and words

PHONICS SKILLS I

Initial consonant: r

Print the letters and words.

R R

r r

ring ring

rain rain

Finish the picture. Finish the word.

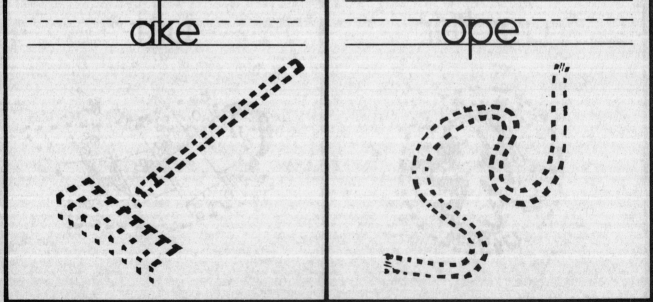

ake

ope

Skills: Recognition of the initial consonant "r"; Writing letters and words; Association between sounds, symbols, and words

PHONICS SKILLS I

Initial consonant: s

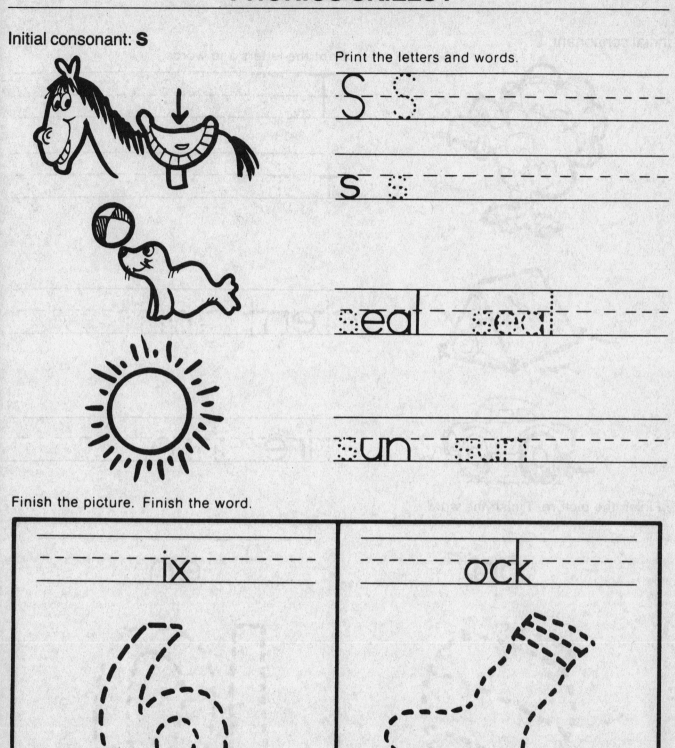

Print the letters and words.

S S

s s

seat seat

sun sun

Finish the picture. Finish the word.

ix

ock

Skills: Recognition of the initial consonant "s"; Writing letters and words; Association between sounds, symbols, and words

PHONICS SKILLS I

Initial consonant: **t**

Print the letters and words.

tent tent

tire tire

Finish the picture. Finish the word.

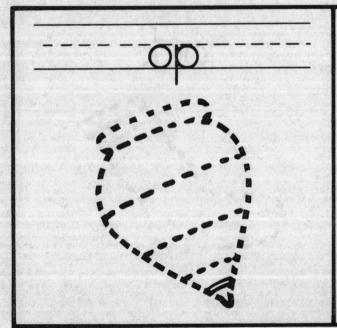

op

en

Skills: Recognition of the initial consonant "t"; Writing letters and words; Association between sounds, symbols, and words

PHONICS SKILLS I

Final consonant: **b**

crab

b   b

Which ones end with **b**? Color them orange. Color the other pictures blue.

Skills: Recognition of the final consonant "b"; Auditory discrimination; Writing the letter "b"; Sound/symbol association

PHONICS SKILLS I

Final consonant: **d**

Which ones end with **d**? Color them yellow. Color the other pictures red.

Skills: Recognition of the final consonant "d"; Auditory discrimination; Writing the letter "d"; Sound/symbol association

96

PHONICS SKILLS I

Final consonant: **g**

Which ones end with **g**? Color them brown. Color the other pictures blue.

Skills: Recognition of the final consonant "g"; Auditory discrimination; Writing the letter "g"; Sound/symbol association

PHONICS SKILLS I

Final consonant: **k**

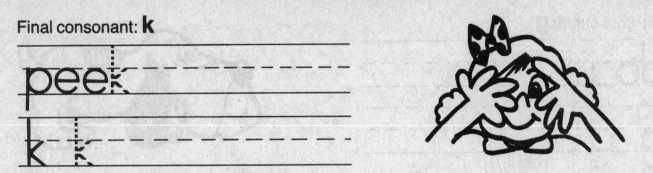

peek

k

Which ones end with **k**? Color them blue. Color the other pictures red.

Skills: Recognition of the final consonant "k"; Auditory discrimination; Writing the letter "k"; Sound/symbol association

PHONICS SKILLS I

Final consonant: **m**

drum

m m

Which ones end with **m**? Color them orange. Color the other pictures red.

Skills: Recognition of the final consonant "m"; Auditory discrimination; Writing the letter "m"; Sound/symbol association

PHONICS SKILLS I

Final consonant: **n**

lion

n

Which ones end with **n**? Color them green. Color the other pictures yellow.

Skills: Recognition of the final consonant "n"; Auditory discrimination; Writing the letter "n"; Sound/symbol association

PHONICS SKILLS I

Final consonant: **p**

jeep

p p

Which ones end with **p**? Color them red. Color the other pictures green.

Skills: Recognition of the final consonant "p"; Auditory discrimination; Writing the letter "p"; Sound/symbol association

101

PHONICS SKILLS I

Final consonant: **r**

bear

r r

Which ones end with **r**? Color them brown. Color the other pictures green.

Skills: Recognition of the final consonant "r"; Auditory discrimination; Writing the letter "r"; Sound/symbol association

PHONICS SKILLS I

Final consonant: **t**

goat

t

Which ones end with **t**? Color them yellow. Color the other pictures blue.

Skills: Recognition of the final consonant "t"; Auditory discrimination; Writing the letter "t"; Sound/symbol association

PHONICS SKILLS I

Final consonant: **X**

fox

x x

Which ones end with **x**? Color them green. Color the other pictures brown.

Skills: Recognition of the final consonant "x"; Auditory discrimination; Writing the letter "x"; Sound/symbol association

PHONICS SKILLS II

Short vowel: ă

A

a

Which ones have the ă sound? Color them blue. Color the other pictures green.

Skills: Recognition of the short vowel "a"; Auditory discrimination; Writing the letter "a"; Sound/symbol association

PHONICS SKILLS II

Short vowel: ĕ

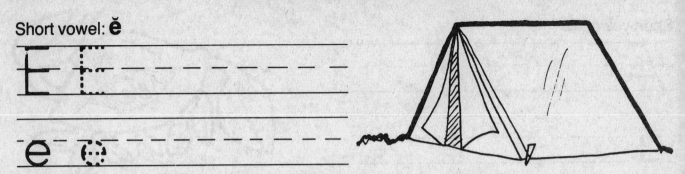

Which ones have the ĕ sound? Color them blue. Color the other pictures yellow.

Skills: Recognition of the short vowel "e"; Auditory discrimination; Writing the letter "e"; Sound/symbol association

PHONICS SKILLS II

Short vowel: ĭ

Which ones have the ĭ sound? Color them green. Color the other pictures brown.

Skills: Recognition of the short vowel "i"; Auditory discrimination; Writing the letter "i"; Sound/symbol association

PHONICS SKILLS II

Short vowel: ŏ

Which ones have the ŏ sound? Color them orange. Color the other pictures green.

Skills: Recognition of the short vowel "o"; Auditory discrimination; Writing the letter "o"; Sound/symbol association

PHONICS SKILLS II

Short vowel: ǔ

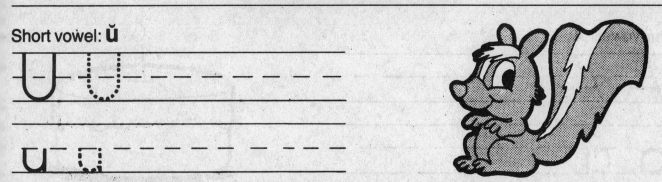

Which ones have the **ǔ** sound? Color them red. Color the other pictures yellow.

Skills: Recognition of the short vowel "u"; Auditory discrimination; Writing the letter "u";
Sound/symbol association

PHONICS SKILLS II

Long vowel: ā

Which ones have the ā sound? Color them red. Color the other pictures blue.

Skills: Recognition of the long vowel "a"; Auditory discrimination; Writing the letter "a"; Sound/symbol association

PHONICS SKILLS II

Long vowel: ē

E ¦-¦- - - - - - - - - - - - -

e ⊙ - - - - - - - - - - - - - -

Which ones have the ē sound? Color them green. Color the other pictures blue.

Skills: Recognition of the long vowel "e"; Auditory discrimination; Writing the letter "e"; Sound/symbol association

PHONICS SKILLS II

Long vowel: **Ī**

Which ones have the **Ī** sound? Color them yellow. Color the other pictures red.

Skills: Recognition of the long vowel "i"; Auditory discrimination; Writing the letter "i"; Sound/symbol association

PHONICS SKILLS II

Long vowel: **ō**

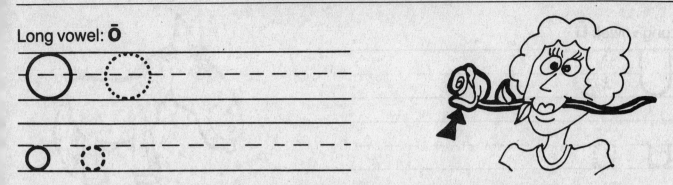

Which ones have the **ō** sound? Color them brown. Color the other pictures blue.

Skills: Recognition of the long vowel "o"; Auditory discrimination; Writing the letter "o"; Sound/symbol association

PHONICS SKILLS II

Long vowel: **ū**

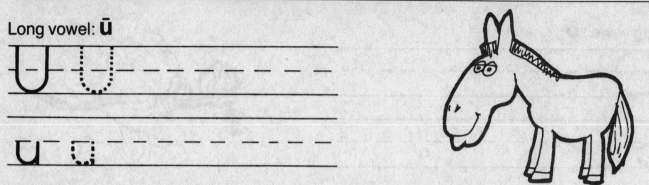

Which ones have the **ū** sound? Color them green. Color the other pictures red.

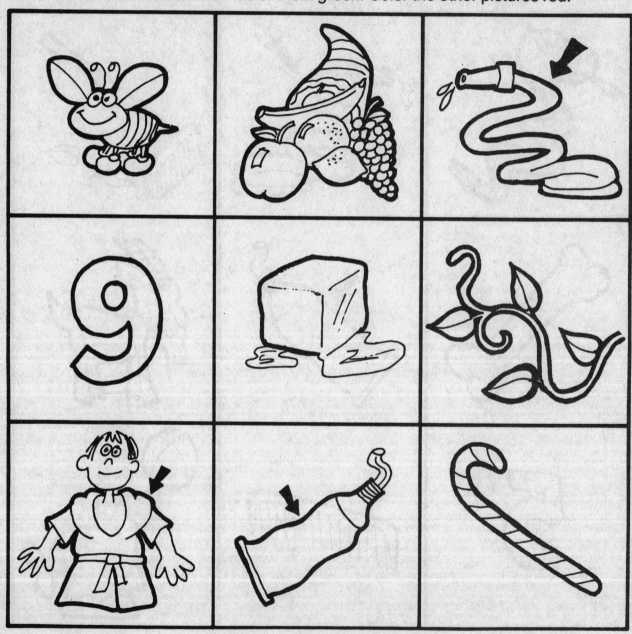

Skills: Recognition of the long vowel "u"; Auditory discrimination; Writing the letter "u"; Sound/symbol association

PHONICS SKILLS II

Long and short vowel: **a**

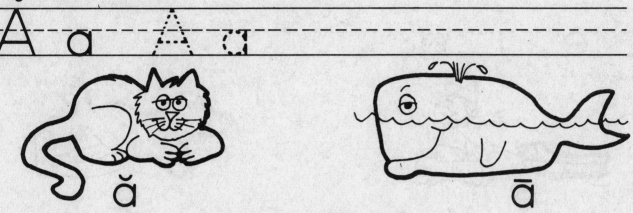

Which ones have the **ă** sound? Color them red.
Which ones have the **ā** sound? Color them blue.

Skills: Auditory and visual discrimination; Sound/symbol association; Writing the letter "a"

PHONICS SKILLS II

Long and short vowel: **e**

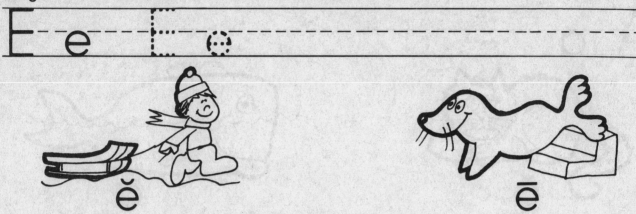

Which ones have the **ĕ** sound? Color them green.
Which ones have the **ē** sound? Color them yellow.

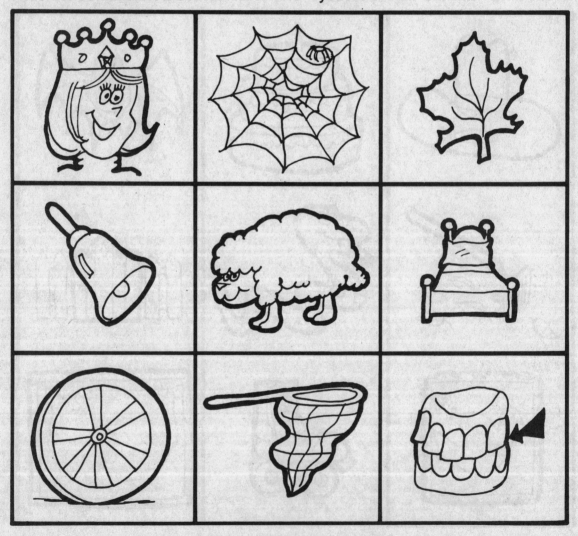

Skills: Auditory and visual discrimination; Sound/symbol association; Writing the letter "e"

PHONICS SKILLS II

Long and short vowel: **i**

I̶ i̶ I̶ i̶ - - - - - - - - - - - - - -

Which ones have the **ĭ** sound? Color them orange.
Which ones have the **ī** sound? Color them yellow.

Skills: Auditory and visual discrimination; Sound/symbol association; Writing the letter "i"

PHONICS SKILLS II

Long and short vowel: O

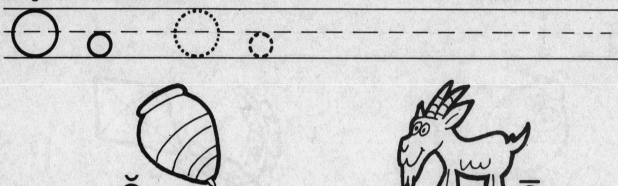

Which ones have the ŏ sound? Color them blue.
Which ones have the ō sound? Color them green.

Skills: Auditory and visual discrimination; Sound/symbol association; Writing the letter "o"

PHONICS SKILLS II

Long and short vowel: **u**

Ŭ Ŭ ŭ Ŭ ŭ

ŭ

ū

Which ones have the **ŭ** sound? Color them green.
Which ones have the **ū** sound? Color them red.

Skills: Auditory and visual discrimination; Sound/symbol association; Writing the letter "u"

PHONICS SKILLS II

Initial consonant blends: **cl, cr**

cl

cr

Which ones begin with **cl**? Color them blue.
Which ones begin with **cr**? Color them green.

Skills: Understanding that some consonant sounds can be blended together;
Sound/symbol association

PHONICS SKILLS II

Initial consonant blends: **bl, br**

b̶l̶ - - - - - - - - - - - - - - -

b̶r̶ - - - - - - - - - - - - - - -

Which ones begin with **bl**? Color them black.
Which ones begin with **br**? Color them brown.

Skills: Understanding that some consonant sounds can be blended together;
Sound/symbol association

PHONICS SKILLS II

Initial consonant blends: **dr, tr**

dr

tr

Which ones begin with **dr**? Color them blue.
Which ones begin with **tr**? Color them red.

Skills: Understanding that some consonant sounds can be blended together;
Sound/symbol association

PHONICS SKILLS II

Initial consonant blends: **sk, sl**

sk - - - - - - - - - -

sl - - - - - - - - - -

Which ones begin with **sk**? Color them yellow.
Which ones begin with **sl**? Color them red.

Skills: Understanding that some consonant sounds can be blended together;
Sound/symbol association

PHONICS SKILLS II

Initial consonant blends: **st, sp**

sp

st

Which ones begin with **sp**? Color them yellow.
Which ones begin with **st**? Color them orange.

Skills: Understanding that some consonant sounds can be blended together;
Sound/symbol association

PHONICS SKILLS II

Initial consonant blends: **fl, fr**

Print the letters and words.

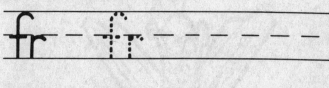

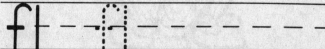

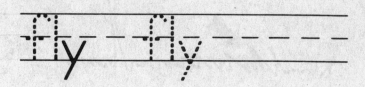

Finish the picture.   Finish the word.

og

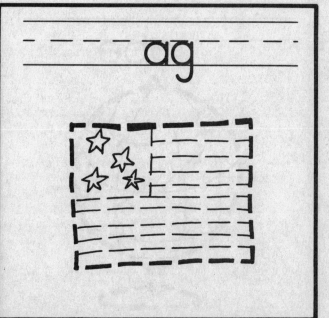

ag

Skills: Understanding that some consonant sounds can be blended together;
Sound/symbol association

PHONICS SKILLS II

Initial consonant blends: **gl, gr**

Print the letters and words.

gr gr

gl gl

grass grass

glove glove

Finish the picture.   Finish the word.

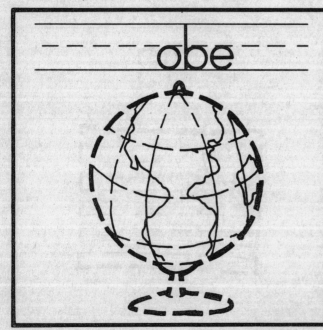

_obe

_apes

Skills: Understanding that some consonant sounds can be blended together; Sound/symbol association

PHONICS SKILLS II

Initial consonant blends: **pl, pr**

Print the letters and words.

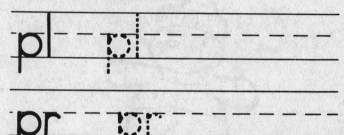

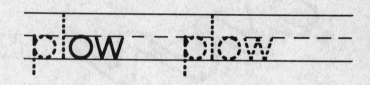

Finish the picture.   Finish the word.

ug

ize

Skills: Understanding that some consonant sounds can be blended together;
Sound/symbol association

PHONICS SKILLS II

Initial consonant blends: **sn, sw**

Print the letters and words.

sn   sn

sw   sw

snake   snake

swan   swan

Finish the picture.   Finish the word.

ail

ing

Skills: Understanding that some consonant sounds can be blended together; Sound/symbol association